Contents

Let's Celebrate!.. 4

A Viking Festival.. 6

Chinese New Year 8

The Festival of Holi... 10

Cherry Blossom Time.. 12

Celebrating Eid-ul-Fitr 14

The Naadam Festival... 16

The Cattle Crossing 18

Happy Thanksgiving! 20

Map: Where in the World? 22

Glossary 23

Index, Learn More Online 24

Words shown in **bold** in the text are explained in the glossary.

All the places in this book are shown on the map on page 22.

Let's Celebrate!

Every year, thousands of different celebrations take place around the world.

During the eight days of Hanukkah, Jews celebrate by lighting candles and giving gifts.

These children in Malaysia are giving a gift to their neighbour at Christmas.

Children and adults dress up to take part in carnivals.

Carnival costumes in Switzerland

On the Day of the Dead in Mexico people take part in parades wearing costumes with skull faces. They take candles, food and flowers to the graves of their loved ones.

In Australia, Aborigines celebrate their history and **culture** during the Laura Aboriginal Dance Festival.

A Viking Festival

In Lerwick on the Shetland Islands, the new year begins with the Up Helly Aa festival.

About 1000 years ago, these Scottish islands were home to **Vikings**.

Up Helly Aa celebrates this history.

Hundreds of people dressed as Vikings parade through the town carrying burning torches.

At the end of the parade, the Vikings march around a huge model of a Viking ship. Then they throw their torches onto the wooden ship and set it on fire.

Chinese New Year

Chinese New Year takes place in late January or early February.

At New Year, Chinese people celebrate new beginnings.

They wear new clothes and clean their homes to sweep away bad luck.

A special New Year meal

Children receive gifts of small red envelopes that contain money.

New Year parades take place in cities around the world. The parades include dancers carrying large dragons. The dragon is a **symbol** of good luck to Chinese people.

A Chinese New Year parade in San Francisco, in the United States

The Festival of Holi

In India, the arrival of spring is celebrated with the festival of Holi.

It is also known as the festival of colour.

Powdered paint for sale in a market during Holi

During Holi, people throw powdered paint and coloured water at each other in the streets.

Kids throw paint at adults and it's even OK to throw paint at strangers!

Holi is a Hindu celebration. It is said that when the Hindu god Krishna was a little boy, he threw coloured water over milkmaids who were milking cows.

Cherry Blossom Time

In Japan, people know that spring has arrived when pink and white blossoms appear on cherry trees.

Cherry blossom

Enjoying a cherry blossom picnic

People gather in parks to see the cherry blossoms.

Families and friends eat picnics under the trees as blossoms gently fall on them.

The Japanese **custom** of visiting parks and gardens to see and enjoy the cherry blossoms is called *hanami*. It means 'flower viewing'.

A night-time hanami party

13

Celebrating Eid-ul-Fitr

Ramadan is the holiest month of the year for Muslims.

During Ramadan, people say extra prayers and try to give up bad habits.

They also fast, or don't eat, between sunrise and sunset.

Muslims celebrate the end of Ramadan with a big festival called Eid-ul-Fitr.

The greeting *Eid Mubarak* means 'blessed Eid'.

On the first day of Eid-ul-Fitr, families and friends gather to eat a special daytime meal. People wear their best clothes and children receive presents. People also give money to those living in poverty.

Children in Pakistan enjoying Eid-ul-Fitr

The Naadam Festival

When summer comes around in Mongolia, it's time for Naadam.

Naadam festivals, or games, are held throughout Mongolia.

Each festival begins with a big parade.

Then competitors take part in wrestling, archery and horse racing competitions.

An archery competition

A wrestling competition

Some of the Naadam horse races are 27 km long. All the jockeys, or riders, are children. Some of the riders are just five years old!

17

The Cattle Crossing

The Fulani people of Mali, in Africa, are cattle **herders**.

For most of the year, many Fulani men live a long way from home.

They walk from place to place, finding grass for their animals.

In December, the herders and thousands of cattle return home by crossing the Niger River.

A young herder swimming across the river with his cattle

The herders' families gather on the riverbank to welcome them home.

The time of the cattle crossing is a great celebration for Fulani families. Everyone celebrates with music, dancing and feasting.

Happy Thanksgiving!

Every November, people all over the United States celebrate Thanksgiving.

In 1621, the **Pilgrims** and their Native American neighbours shared a feast to celebrate a good harvest.

Americans think of this as the first Thanksgiving.

A parade is held in New York every Thanksgiving.

Today, American families still enjoy a Thanksgiving feast of turkey, stuffing, cranberry sauce, sweet potatoes and pumpkin pie.

Not everyone has a place to live or enough food. Every Thanksgiving, helpers at homeless shelters cook Thanksgiving dinners for people living in poverty.

Where in the World?

Shetland Islands, Scotland
Pages 6-7

Switzerland
Page 5

Israel
Page 4

Mongolia
Pages 16–17

Japan
Pages 12–13

North America

Europe

Asia

China
Page 8

United States
Pages 9 and 20–21

Africa

South America

Australia

Malaysia
Page 4

Mexico
Page 5

Mali
Pages 18–19

Pakistan
Page 15

India
Pages 10–11 and 14

Australia
Page 5

Glossary

culture
The beliefs and way of life of a group of people. For example, celebrations, food and clothes are all part of a group's culture.

custom
A particular action or way of doing something that has not changed in many years.

herder
A person who herds, or moves, animals from place to place so that the animals can find food.

Pilgrims
People who left England in 1620 and settled in the part of the world that is now the United States.

symbol
An item, picture or sign that stands for something else. Dragons are symbols of good luck to Chinese people.

Vikings
People who lived about 1000 years ago. They came from Norway, Sweden and Denmark. The Vikings were sailors and warriors.

Index

A
Aboriginal people 5

C
cattle crossing 18–19
cherry blossoms 12–13
Chinese New Year 8–9
Chinese people 8–9
Christmas 4

D
Day of the Dead 5

E
Eid-ul-Fitr 14–15

F
Fulani people 18–19

H
Hanukkah 4
Hindu people 10–11
Holi 10–11

J
Japanese people 12–13
Jewish people 4

L
Laura Aboriginal Dance
  Festival 5

M
Muslim people 14–15

N
Naadam festival 16–17

P
parades 5, 6–7, 9, 16, 20

T
Thanksgiving 20–21

U
Up Helly Aa festival 6–7

V
Vikings 6–7

Learn More Online

To learn more about celebrations
around the world, go to
www.rubytuesdaybooks.com/celebrations